Rubbish Truck

Annabel Savery

W
FRANKLIN WATTS
LONDON·SYDNEY

First published in 2009 by
Franklin Watts
338 Euston Road
London NW1 3BH

Franklin Watts Australia
Level 17/207 Kent Street
Sydney NSW 2000

© 2009 Franklin Watts

ISBN: 978 0 7496 9292 6

Dewey classification number: 629.2'24

A CIP catalogue record for this book is available
from the British Library.

Planning and production by Discovery Books Limited
Managing editor: Rachel Tisdale
Editor: Annabel Savery
Designer: Ian Winton

Acknowledgements: Alamy: pp. 7 & 30 (David Kilpatrick), 8 (Peter Bennett), 17 (Jeff
Smith), 19 (Ros Drinkwater); Biffa Waste Services, 2008: pp. 4, 12, 14 top, 18, 22; DAF: cover
main & title, p. 16; Discovery Photo Library: p. 23 (Chris Fairclough); Dreamstime: p. 27
(Vadkoz); Farid UK Limited: p. 24; Alan Fuller Ltd.: p. 28; Istockphoto.com: cover top right
& 25, pp. 5 (Mike Clarke), 9 (Mike Clarke); Johnston Sweepers Limited: pp. 20, 21 both;
Norman D. Large: p. 6; Photolibrary: p. 26 (Inga Spence); S.C. Fabrications (Norwich)
Ltd.: p. 29; Scania: p. 11; Shutterstock: pp. 10 (Daniel Goodchild), 13 (Vadimkozlovsky),
15 (Zygimantas Cepaitis); Volvo: cover top left & p. 14 bottom.

Printed in China

Franklin Watts is a division of Hachette Children's Books, an Hachette UK company.
www.hachette.co.uk

Contents

What are rubbish trucks?

Lots of rubbish is produced by homes and businesses every day. A rubbish truck is used to collect this rubbish and take it away.

The rubbish truck has a big container on the back. This can be filled with all kinds of rubbish.

There are many types of rubbish truck. They are designed to empty bins and collect different types of waste.

Some trucks collect huge loads of rubbish; others collect very small loads.

Rubbish truck fact!
Some rubbish trucks have space for 27 cubic metres of rubbish – that's enough space for 10,000 full boxes of cereal.

Parts of a rubbish truck

Look at all the parts on a rubbish truck.
Do you know what they are all for?

There are different types of rubbish truck.

This is a **front loader**.

Forks
Long spikes on the lifting equipment of a front loader. They are used to pick up heavy bins.

Lifting equipment
A device that is used to lift bins.

Body
The main back part of the rubbish truck.

Wheels

Lights

Rubbish truck fact!

A rubbish truck has the same base as a truck. Then the body is added to make it a rubbish truck.

This is a **rear loader**.

Cab
The rubbish truck driver sits in the cab.

Hopper
The big space in the body that rubbish is tipped into.

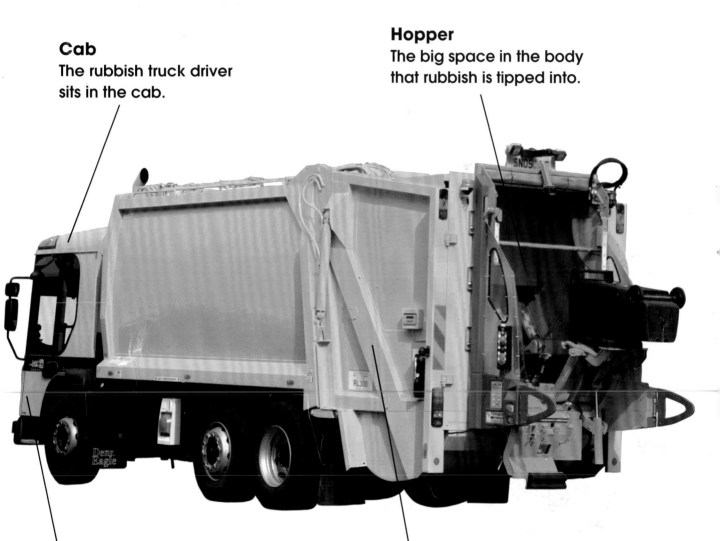

Engine
A rubbish truck has a big, powerful engine.

Tailgate
The back part of the body that lifts up.

The hopper

The hopper is a very important part of the rubbish truck. This is where all the rubbish is put.

Rubbish bins are attached to lifting equipment on the front, side or back of the body.

The bins are lifted and tipped up so that their contents empty into the hopper.

Rubbish truck fact!
Bins come in all shapes and sizes depending on what type of rubbish is being collected. One city in the UK has purple bins.

Rubbish is tipped into the hopper.
Then a big piece of metal, called
the **packing blade**, squashes all
the rubbish up to one end.

Packing blade

This makes space for the next lot of rubbish
to be emptied into the hopper.

The cab and the engine

The driver sits in the cab to drive the rubbish truck.

There is space for crew members in the cab too. Crew members, called **loaders**, get out of the cab to attach bins to the lifting equipment.

Cab

The loaders must have time to load and empty all the bins, so the rubbish truck driver drives along very slowly.

Engine

The engine creates power
to drive the rubbish truck along.
It must be powerful because the
body is very heavy when it is full.

The engine runs on **fuel**, just like a car engine.

Rubbish truck fact!
Some rubbish trucks are now powered by electricity.

Front loaders

A front loader is a type of rubbish truck. It has two forks on the front. These are used to lift bins and empty rubbish into the hopper.

Forks

The front loader picks up big rubbish containers from businesses. These containers have **sleeves** on each side.

Sleeve

Hopper

The forks slide into the sleeves. Then the forks are raised and the bin is lifted up. The lid of the bin opens and the rubbish falls out.

Rubbish truck fact!
Some front loaders can be operated by one person.

13

Rear loaders

Rear loaders are mainly used to collect household waste. They empty **wheely bins** and collect bin bags from outside houses.

Rear loaders have lifting equipment at the back. Wheely bins are hooked on to it and lifted up. The bin tips as it is lifted.

Wheely bin

As it is tipped up the bin lid opens. The rubbish falls out into the hopper.

The loaders operate the lifting equipment from the back of the truck.

Rubbish truck fact!
Some rubbish trucks can be loaded from the side.

Collecting rubbish

A rubbish collection route starts very early in the morning, before many people are awake!

The crew drive along streets and collect the bins from outside each house.

The loaders walk behind or in front of the rubbish truck collecting the bins, emptying them and putting them back outside the houses.

When the hopper is full the crew drive
the rubbish truck to the **landfill
site**. Here they empty
the rubbish.

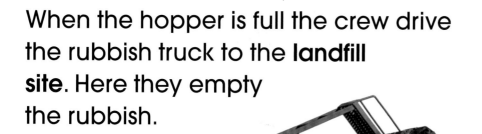

Tailgate

The back section of the body is called the tailgate.
This lifts up and the rubbish is emptied out.

Rubbish truck fact!
Big rubbish trucks will make two trips a day to
the landfill site.

Skip trucks

When people need to collect a lot of rubbish they might use a skip. This is a big, open container that has lots of space for all kinds of rubbish.

The skip is delivered and taken away on a skip truck. A skip truck has special equipment for lifting skips.

The skip truck has two arms on the back. These have chains attached to them. The chains are attached to hooks on the side of the skip.

Once the chains are connected, the two arms move backwards or forwards. As they move they lift the skip up in the air. The arms keep moving until the skip is either over the back of the truck or over the ground. Then the skip is lowered.

Road sweeper trucks

Road sweeper trucks are used to clean roads and pavements.

They have two round brushes underneath the cab at the front, or under the body.

Rubbish truck fact!

Road sweepers have two engines – one to power the truck and one to power the sweeping equipment.

As the road sweeper drives along, the brushes spin. They sweep any rubbish on the road underneath the machine. Here, it is sucked up into a container in the back of the sweeper.

Brushes

Some road sweepers also have a hose. The **operator** can use this to suck up rubbish in places that the brushes cannot reach.

Hose

Recycling trucks

Recycling trucks are used to collect rubbish
that can be **recycled**. This might be
glass, plastic, cardboard,
paper or metal.

Recyclable rubbish is put out to be collected in
the same way as other rubbish. The recycling
truck then drives around to collect it.

Some recycling trucks have separate compartments for different materials. The loaders sort the rubbish into the compartments, instead of throwing it all in together.

When the recycling truck is full, it is taken to the **recycling centre**. Here, each type of material goes into a separate container to be recycled.

Rubbish truck fact!

There are recycling trucks that collect food waste too. This is made into **compost**.

Small rubbish trucks

Small rubbish trucks look like the larger rubbish trucks, but they are half the size.

They can travel through narrow streets and small lanes. They are used to collect rubbish from houses that larger rubbish trucks cannot reach.

Road sweeper trucks can also be very small. They are used to sweep and polish surfaces that cannot be driven on by a big road sweeper.

Rubbish truck fact!
Small rubbish trucks can weigh seven tonnes when they are empty and eleven when they are full.

Big rubbish trucks

On the longest routes, big rubbish trucks must be used. They can collect as much as 12 tonnes of rubbish before they go to the landfill site.

Big rubbish trucks are very heavy.
When they are full they can weigh
26 tonnes. That's the same as 27 cars!

Rubbish truck fact!

Big front loaders can lift containers that weigh over three tonnes.

Big rubbish trucks need lots of wheels.
They help to support the heavy truck
as it drives along.

Special rubbish trucks

Some businesses produce liquid waste. This needs to be collected in a special rubbish truck.

Liquid waste, such as oil, can be taken away in a **vacuum** tanker. This is a truck with a big **sealed** container on the back.

Grab trucks are used when there is a lot of
rubbish to collect, or the rubbish is very big
or heavy.

Trailer

The grab truck has a big, open trailer and a
long arm attached behind the cab. The arm
picks up the rubbish and drops it into the trailer.

Rubbish truck fact!
Vacuum tankers can carry up to 6,000 litres of liquid.

Rubbish truck activities

Art: Design a poster to encourage people to recycle more. You can use old materials to make your poster.

Literacy: Imagine that you are mistakenly collected by the rubbish truck! Write a story about your journey to the landfill site and how you would escape.

Science: Lots of rubbish is tipped into landfill sites every day. What type of rubbish do you think lasts longest?

Geography: Think about all the homes and businesses around the world. How much rubbish do you think they all produce in a day? How do you think they could reduce their waste?

Design & Technology: Design and make a model of a rubbish truck. You can use lots of old materials to do this.

Glossary

body the main back part of the rubbish truck

compost a mixture of rotting plants

forks two spikes at the front of a front loader that are used to lift rubbish containers

front loader a rubbish truck with lifting equipment at the front

fuel liquid that is used to power a vehicle's engine

hopper the space in the body that rubbish is tipped into

landfill site a large hole in the ground where rubbish is buried

lifting equipment a device on a rubbish truck that lifts rubbish bins and empties them into the hopper

loaders rubbish truck crew members

operator the person who controls a vehicle's attachments

packing blade a large piece of metal that squashes the rubbish in the rubbish truck up to one end

rear loader a rubbish truck with lifting equipment at the back

recycle to process old materials to turn them into new products

recycling centre a place where different materials are collected and recycled

sealed closed tightly

sleeve the part on the side of a large rubbish container that the forks slide into

tailgate the back part of a rubbish truck that lifts up

vacuum a sealed space from which air has been removed

wheely bin a plastic or metal container for rubbish, which has wheels on the bottom

Further information

Recycling Operative (When I'm at Work), Sue Barraclough, Franklin Watts, 2006

Rubbish and Recycling (Earth in Danger), Helen Orme, ticktock Media Ltd., 2008.

The Recycling Centre (Out and About), Sue Barraclough, Franklin Watts, 2009.

The Stinking Story of Rubbish, Katie Daynes, Usborne Publishing Ltd., 2006.

This is my Truck (Mega Machine Drivers), Chris Oxlade, Franklin Watts, 2006.

Trucks (Big Machines), David and Penny Glover, Franklin Watts, 2007.

Index